BLACK SEA

Books by David Yezzi

Birds of the Air
Tomorrow & Tomorrow
Azores
Sad Is Eros
The Hidden Model

As editor
The Swallow Anthology of New American Poets

BLACK SEA

DAVID YEZZI

Carnegie Mellon University Press
Pittsburgh 2018

ACKNOWLEDGMENTS

Thanks to the editors of the following journals, in which these poems first appeared, occasionally in different versions:

32 Poems: "New Town," "The Rock Balancer"
Academic Questions: "The Able Man"
Academy of American Poets *Poem-a-Day*: "Living Room," "Meditation"
The American Journal of Poetry: "Low Ceiling"
The Atlantic: "Weeds," "Paper Whites"
Barrow Street: "The Consolations"
Cocytus: "Tomis"
E-Verse Radio: "Capgras"
Light: "The Faculty Abroad"
Literary Matters: "The Double Deuce"
New Ohio Review: "Night Blind," "Aubade," "Let," "Hooked"
Parnassus: Poetry in Review: "Stalker"
Partisan: "Truepenny"
PN Review: "Old Friends," "Last Job"
Sewanee Theological Review: "The Chain," "Thud"
Smartish Pace: "Crush," "On the Death of a Houseplant," "Plague"
Smithsonian: "Café Future"
The Yale Review: "Dying the Day Prince Died"

"Plague" was included in *Resistance, Rebellion, Life: 50 Poems Now* (Knopf), edited by Amit Majmudar.

"Pan Am" was included in *Rabbit Ears: TV Poems* (NYQ Books), edited by Joel Allegretti.

"Thud" and "The Hug" were printed in fine-press editions by Aralia Press.

Book design by Kate Martin

Library of Congress Control Number 2017950740
ISBN 978-0-88748-635-7
Copyright © 2018 David Yezzi
Printed and bound in the United States of America

10   9   8   7   6   5   4   3   2   1

Contents

for Sarah

I have beaten out my exile.
—"Lustra," Ezra Pound

Who in his mind has not probed the black water?
—*East of Eden*, John Steinbeck

1

NIGHT BLIND

There's a spot
at the top
of the street,
where the lamp

is out, that's
the darkest
part of the
block. I don't

go that way
at night, though
it would be
all right,

I know. No one's
there, just
a chained-up dog
in damp air

and branches
too dark to see,
like black water
churning.

LIVING ROOM

God sees me. I see you. You're just like me.
　　This is the cul-de-sac I've longed to live on.
Pure-white and dormered houses sit handsomely

along the slate-roofed, yew-lined neighborhood.
　　Past there is where my daughters walk to school,
across the common rounded by a wood.

And in my great room, a modest TV
　　informs me how the earth is grown so small,
ringed by spice routes of connectivity.

My father lived and died in his same chair
　　and kept it to one beer. There's good in that.
Who could look down upon, or even dare

to question, what he managed out of life?
　　Age makes us foolish. Still, he had a house,
a patch of grass and room to breathe, a wife.

It's my house now, and I do as I please.
　　I bless his name. I edge the yard, plant greens.
Our girls swing on the porch in a coming breeze.

Café Future

The bunting they put out for the grand opening
never got put away, so every day

looks as if it might be opening day.
You inquire if Café Future carries pie,

and sure enough it's right there on the menu.
A slice of rhubarb and black coffee, please.

The pie tastes like you'd hoped it would, but sweeter.
And though you're wary of newfangledness,

you've never had a piece of pie this good.
You think you'll make the Future your new place.

The long counter's reflected in plate glass,
where sunlight pours in from the parking lot,

and the guy who's looking back at you is you
and not quite you. The morning rush is over.

The chrome gleams with a perfect gleaminess.
The waitress's smile lets you know she agrees.

It makes you want to stay and eat more pie.
She comes by, young looking, like her own daughter,

and whisks your plate away. Another slice.
I know I really shouldn't. Just one more.

That's fine with her, she says. She's on a double
and happy to bring you pie all day long.

THE CHAIN

Outside Giant,
a woman, whose child—
one of three, all under ten,
and this one maybe five,
a girl—is going wild,
crying (keening really),
up the canned goods aisle,
past the Wonder,
crazed, noncompliant,
face borscht red,

now breaks down
herself—the mom, I mean—
grabbing the kid by the coat.
She pulls her close and screams
something PG-13
in the half-full parking lot,
not caring that we've seen
her lose her shit.
Two cars down,
a guy, foot-lit

by tail lights,
starts tsking as he pops his trunk,
saying good and loud, for me to hear,
"That's no way to treat your kid."
He wobbles like he's drunk
or has bad hips, slides
into his piece of junk
and turns it over.
His brights
illuminate the river

of rain
bubbling like sea spray
across the pocked anchorage

in which our cars are moored.
          On my way
home, it's still needling me:
What's with that guy? Okay,
          he has no children. But who's
               more insane?
          He's sure it's her; I choose

          him. And me?
          Tonight my son
actually flinches as he turns
the corner, still stinging from my swat,
          with his Nerf gun
cocked. He paints the enemy,
remembering him red-faced, gone
          ballistic, flashing teeth.
               Down his sights, he
          squints and aims at me.

          And I agree:
          they will be in his mind
forever, the image of me raging
and the look on his mother's face.
          Will he, in his turn, find
a different way to be? So far,
he is, in his finer moments, kind.
          Other times he'll turn
               raw, like me, and like me
          will not learn.

NEW TOWN

The storm-light and the blowing bales of leaves,
mountainous clouds, the frequent gusts of rain,
humidity that makes him sweat at night:
this wasn't the way it was in the old town.

In homeroom he has to stand without a desk
until a teacher sends him to his place.
When she says his name, thirty faces turn,
and when they look away they don't look back.

His father's still living in the other place.
His mother has appointments during the day.
When he gets home he microwaves a plate
and empties a can for the cat. They eat.

In the dark, his mother, home by eight, can see
the TV beaming through the picture window,
as he paces through a dungeon with a rifle
and fires in an indiscriminate spray

at anything that moves. His mother lies
down with her clothes still on. Soon, she will sleep.
The porch light shows bare trees above the yard
and the rusty sumac in a low-slung sky.

Weeds

My emerald legions, how tall you have grown:
so many. With what supernatural speed

you overlord the weakest in the garden—
frizzled hydrangeas, sere mint, sun-starved basil.

Tousle-headed, you can see the sky
above the cowering, defeated plots.

This is your day of triumph: eager sugars
rise up through your ramifying stalks.

And I allowed it. My cool inattention
found good reasons to look the other way,

since all that grows is good, or so I thought.
How soon would height recall high thoughts, and yet,

if I uproot you now, how I would miss you.
Sweet knotgrass, heartsick briar, purple thistle.

Even tilled up, the garden wouldn't look
as it did when my grandmother warned me

not to grow too fast. She lived to be
a hundred, girlhood lost except for this:

a vague lightness coming, as though of wings
lifting her above the loamy soil,

and all she thought of, as the wind upheld her,
was the packed ground, how tenuous her flight.

Or so I imagine. Though half her age,
I, too, can't quite remember what it felt like

to be light-footed, open to the sun,
without the clogging stems elbowing out

what I meant when I first planted here:
larkspur, geraniums, cilantro, lime.

DYING THE DAY PRINCE DIED

                          is the opposite of being born
on the same day as, say, Marie Curie or Bach
or even Prince, for that matter, or the artist
formerly known as The Artist Formerly Known
As Prince. Now, just Prince, as he will
forever be known. Too bad I never met him.
You, I met. A few times, as a matter of fact,
but you never remembered my ever meeting you.
Memory's a tricky thing, and so I forgive you.
Who am I, after all? Just a person, with a pulse.
A pulse is good, particularly from your perspective,
I'd imagine. The internet is burning up with the news
of Prince's death, almost literally on fire
with the heat generated by his solo on the all-star
"While My Guitar Gently Weeps" at the Rock and Roll
Hall of Fame. At the end, instead of a mic drop,
Prince throws his guitar up in the air, and as far as
we're concerned, watching it on YouTube,
it never comes down, a guitar-chariot of flame,
its stained-ash body somewhere becoming spirit.

I'm not sure where you died or how exactly.
I heard of it through friends. You had been ill.
There hasn't been a whole lot in the press.
It's possible that I missed it, that we missed it.
We've all been so distracted by the passing
of Prince, by our wish to be purified again
in the waters of Lake Minnetonka, by the terror
of a father's drunken rage, by laughter and the rhythmic
click of boots walking in lamplit rain.

THE CONSOLATIONS

In this abandoned house I got to love
telenovelas. Marta slaps the air
a foot from the face of her once-true love.
Jorge's head jerks back from the force of love,
and, in the storm between them, a supercell
rumbles and lows: after the flash of love,
the usual crack, just slightly late. *Amor
Prohibido*, the snowy TV set
warns them—and us. Their fates supremely set,
they drop into the oubliette of love,
head over heels, powerless to counteract
lust's common law, which they soulfully enact.

It doesn't matter that it's all an act;
for me, alone with them, it feels like love.
For desperate lovers, there can be no act
more human than to stumblingly react.
I mouth the words as they fly through the air,
"No sé haría sin ti, mi amore." Both act
the parts that backstairs lovers die to act.
I feel their hurt, its charge, in every cell—
a tongue-tip on a 9-volt Duracell.
Their future, plunging down a cataract,
hides in mist, not clear like at the outset,
upended just as everything was set.

Even with the whip-thin glamorous set,
the turnabout, the unforeseeable act,
a single word, can, in a breath, upset
the plan. *The Wheel of Fortune* has a set
of rules that are decidedly hard to love.
The take-home consolation is a set
of matching steak knives—*Don't adjust your set.
You heard that right. (Are we still on the air?)*
My murmured pleas rise up as thin as air,
a hiss emitted by a wiped cassette.

My food is gone. I have some things to sell.
When they are gone and nothing's left to sell,

the cable will get cut and then my cell.
I sit for six hours at the TV set,
my thoughts a whirligig, a carousel,
one thought in hiding, coiled, a sleeper cell.
On the news tonight: an actor's desperate act.
(I knew him, Horacio.) When does a cell
no longer behave as a healthy cell,
dividing itself for the last time? Love
recedes—as Marta knows—till even love
of comfort and daylight drains off cell by cell.
It's like I'm finally coming up for air
but my lungs burn for something more than air.

Black-and-white movies never go off the air,
and QVC has jewels enough to sell.
A rising generation crowds the air-
waves with its lissome smiles bright as Bel Air.
I dial the hotline. *Busy.* So, I set
the phone down, crack a high window for air.
From here, it's hard to calculate the air
that separates the notion from the act.
I don't remember how I'm supposed to act.
I know now that I cannot live on air.
I know that I no longer live for love.
Pero no se puede vivir sin amar.

The phone is quiet. It's a sign of love.
Friends have all turned their faces from the act.
I cannot move or change the course that's set.
I sound the ardor of the cancer cell,
the mouth that, underwater, gulps at air.

MEDITATION

Take it easy, my Sadness. Settle down.
You asked for evening. Now it's come. It's here.
A choking fog has blanketed the town,
infecting some with calm, the rest with fear.

While the squalid throng of mortals feels the sting
of heartless pleasure swinging its barbed knout
and finds remorse in slavish partying,
take my hand, Sorrow. I will lead you out,

away from them. Look as the dead years lurch
in tattered clothes from heaven's balconies.
From the depths, regret emerges with a grin.

The spent sun passes out beneath an arch,
and, shroudlike, stretched from the antipodes,
—hear it, O hear, love!—soft night marches in.

from the French of Baudelaire

TRAGEDY

That's quite a title that Franz Kline has given
his late-career oil at the BMA.
Those AbEx cats were really serious,
serious drinkers and serious about their art.
Me, I like the title. But look at this thing:
not stygian or glum, knee-deep in blood.
It's all sunny yellows, except for what
is going on there in the center, gray
and brown and black. The eye goes to those later.

First, it's lemons and pinks and blues. And orange.
My god, it's like a sunrise, not a place
where bad things happen. And that's exactly right.
Old Franz Kline knew what he was up to. Sure,
atrocities often root down in the dark.
Ditches make room for limed and fetid bodies.
But they are not the sites of tragedy.
It's when there is no stain of evildoing,
ever. Where poppies overgrow the soil.

Imagine, say, King Lear ceding his kingdom
not in some flinty throne room but a field
surrounded by green hills a league from the sea.
He's dozing in late sunlight, as a few
benign and sluggish bees surround his head.
It's warm. His daughters' robes trail over the grass
and billow like jibs in the saltish breeze.
The nattering of Kent and Gloucester wakes him,
and the king remembers he has work to do.
He rises and strides forward to where a map
the size of a large carpet is unrolled
in blinding light. Sun hits Cordelia's hair;
it blazes yellow. No sign of rain clouds,
and gale-force winds seem unimaginable.
All's perfectly tranquil as the old king
begins to speak of love to his loved daughters.

PLAGUE

Some ancient stories begin with a sickness—
Ilium, Egypt, Thebes. The cause is hidden

from the sufferers, at least for the time being,
though slowly they begin to guess at it.

A mother holds her drowned child in her lap.
A man, to remain a man, is shot to death.

Abandoned and hell-bent, they flee in droves.
Many turn to magic for protection.

And those who foresee red tides get ignored.
The sands, where bodies lie unburied, scroll

past us, in glowing outposts of attention.
Or on nearby streets. Staggering, the number.

What does their ruler—wittingly or not—
keep from them of the evil that began it:

inhuman wrath and blinding counterwrath?
And in the stalled line of midmorning traffic,

each driver views the sky through charcoal glass
and feels just how he has a right to feel.

STALKER

There's a decided lack of flowers in The Zone.
Weeds, sure. And mud. There are no lime-tree bowers in The Zone.

There's a feral dog and lots of poisonous water.
There's three Russians traveling literally for hours in The Zone—

two guys and a close-shorn Stalker (not much of a talker,
that one), on the hunt for mystical powers in The Zone,

whatever those might be. One guy's a writer and super ponderous;
the other's an earnest prof. Why are there no whisky sours in The Zone?

That might liven things up a bit. As it is,
one guy sits brooding, as another cowers in The Zone,

curled up like a fetal pig, surrounded by the detritus of a lost world:
ruined dachas and smashed-up towers in The Zone.

These guys are really filthy, too, and must reek to high heaven.
Is there a law against taking showers in The Zone?

Now someone's gone and made a video game of the film.
There's guns and monsters that the "meatgrinder" devours in The Zone.

And Chernobyl's in the subtitle for pop-toxic effect,
as Andrei's psychic child, gone before me, glowers in The Zone.

2 | BLACK SEA

I | TOMIS

Grousing's
no good.
Chafe won't

make you love
me or ask
me home.

But this bellyaching
snake-charms

my mind, as,
over water on this
new shore,
I look out on
a blank sky.

*

Yesterday
I saw a man—
roofless,

ranting,
with blood
on his head,
half naked—
holding

out his hands
to me, to
god, to dogs.

His eyes flashed red
& white.

No stranger ever
looked at me
like that
before,
as if
suddenly

he saw
someone
he knew.

II | WHITE JASMINE

I must sound like I'm speaking in a foreign language.
    But we adapt. Of course.

    It's not so bad, knowing the names of things,
how to get from home to the harbor, bars

    where they serve drinks laced with absinthe.
Wormwood is for forgetting and early summer.

    A high wind sweeps the stones clean. Each flower
flares briefly like the memory of friends then falls,

    acrid and brown and pasted to the walk.

    A tawny fox wanders the perimeter
of the yard edged with shrubs in bloom & eyes

    birds that perch along the fence.
How easily detail is wrung from the rag of the past,

    no enlivening clues, no tender recognitions,
only the faintest tinge, like a dirty sky at evening, whose

    ochre glow hardly knows it was day.

III | FALSE HOLLY

This waxy
faker
grows everywhere
here, whole

bushes of it,
gem green
trees ranging
overhead

with such
generosity

& élan,
falsehood
flourishing

as if
it were the
the most natural,
God-wanted
thing
in the

world.

IV | PATAPSCO

The water scums up at the edge of the harbor,
evanescing like beer into sawdust.

Behind the black glass of hurtling cars,
the denizens crane forward, tilt their brows,

jaws set, striated muscle at the bone
& in their inner ear a grinding sound.

They're hard as metal. Cold abandonment
has made them *backwater.*

What keeps me up at night is not the fear
that I will never feel that I belong

to them, but that I will.
They have a hollow look,

as if the soul's drained from the body,
but the soul hangs on, hunkered down behind coal eyes.

They hold the road, fly by, not slowing down.
You've missed your turn. You are already lost.

V | THE LONG COAT

I saw you walking away from me
across the brown bricks in your long, black coat.
You haven't worn that coat in years,
not since we moved here, where it's not the fashion.
But there you were, your blond hair comme il faut,
a swim in your step so that the fabric jumped—
such a commanding, youthful figure, such
stride & assurance oh, light, act & balance.
The ground rolled in waves and trees clung to their
last leaves, the ones that had them. It was winter.
And I thought I saw you walking away.

VI | TRUEPENNY

Green light drapes the window
as if air were ivy climbing the bricks
& over the windowsill.
The morning is what it is. Still,

surprising things happen
every day,
walking to work.
Life could change. It's the perk

of living with so much aggression
and trash and trade in misery,
which no one regards or not for very long.
It's a Tin Pan Alley song

that starts out wistful, but then
you're dancing down the street in the rain,
insanely joyful, without the least surprise,
when, suddenly, you realize

there's music pooling in the drains.
I am an echo of the tune I was,
my voice still going on inside,
a ghost crooning to one who's died.

VII | THE DRAIN

Below the wrought-iron grating, water runs
even in dry weather.
                              Tonight it roars
with a sluice of slush & freezing rain,
droning on torrentially into the dark.

House lights blink on, fiercely ocular,
as up the hill the quiet, wooded park's
a wasteland no one wanders in at night.
The streetlamp senses me as I come close.

Underfoot, it makes the sound of going,
already lower down, finding its way
to the stream & then the bay, then out to sea.
It starts from nowhere and leaves rapidly.

VIII | CAPGRAS

We talk
drink wine
joke

sometimes
uproariously
& in
truth

they look
so much
like our friends

the way
their eyes
light up
at the sight of us.

Look, the
low sun agrees,
moving over
their faces this
evening

as the lamps
come on around
the neighbor-
hood

& we
share with them
our stories
& our
plans.

It's as if they've
known us now
forever, as
if we grew up

in this uncanny
valley, where all
our lives they've
loved us all
our lives.

IX | LOW CEILING

The clouds have caused delays. Flights are on hold.
Coming in from the county, traffic stalls
behind an accident we cannot see.
We know it's there & know it must be bad.

We are absolutely stuck. It makes me angry,
makes me want to find the one whose fault
this is. God damn it, damn it, *damn*. I'm fine.
Can't remember if I took my Lexapro.

Or maybe it's because I gave up smoking.
I'm investing in my future. It feels good.
But why are all these duplexes abandoned?
Prejudice just means our minds are made up

beforehand. It's not that we're afraid of failure;
we long ago foresaw all this would fail.
The sky seems grayer than it's ever been.
Windowless façades open on thin air.

And now we're finally moving past the wreck.
Some van with tinted windows slows enough
to look and know *At least it wasn't me,*
cruising over a shoal of raw green gems.

X | AUBADE

I wake up in my old house,
squinting at the seam of light
gilding the flowered curtains,
as six flights down the city's up before me.
Across the street, a woman in green
unchains the gated park. The block
fills with taxis. The light turns,
then turns back without me.

3 |

ON THE DEATH
OF A HOUSEPLANT

My Christmas cactus is dead. Dead. O blameful
house sitter, who cared more for having sex
in my bed with your girlfriend of the hour,
sleeping in and watching Netflix, drinking beer.
Thank you for the briefs you left behind.
I thought I'd wash and wear them as some meager
recompense for the life that you cut short,
but I did not. That plant was hard to kill.
Believe me. When I found it years ago
in the apartment of the girl I later married,
I thought it wouldn't make it. But it struggled
through our dating and our breakup, the engagement—
which, by the way, was wrought by long-stemmed flowers.
It lived though a change of city—twice.
It wouldn't bloom at first and never would,
I thought. But over the years tender new sections,
soft as eyelids, tentatively appeared,
and then, each winter, fuchsia flowers.
Here is the window where it took its light.
The untold thoughts that swirled around my head
like dust motes, as I looked out through the stems
of this familiar friend, I've put away.
It will bloom again in heaven, but never again here.
I blame myself. I was away too long.

HOOKED

She's a friend I take some nights for pain.
Dosage is an issue. We maintain

an equilibrium, but it is hard:
the IV drip of texts, the memory card

of photos we filled one fall by the sea.
What's good for her is mostly good for me,

but pressure points that ease her nerves today
may frazzle them tomorrow. Tough to say;

tough, too, to get just right, or right at all.
Every step's the first part of a fall.

What is this bloodless tie sustaining us,
thumb-pal, app-gal, cyber glamorous,

cobble of connections wormed through space,
which might dissolve if we came face-to-face,

in the flesh, as they say? Now more than ever
this boudoir of electrons echoes *never*—

a touchless ache while it still keeps its feel
that might have ended worse had it been real.

CRUSH

I've never felt like this for anyone.
I bet you get me the way that I get you.

That isn't something people normally do.
Your face zooms floor to ceiling, and I think

I know what it is to have to play a role.
I hope you know that I'm okay with that.

There's a sadness in the curling of your lip.
That runway gown you wore I liked a lot.

I have good taste. You'll get to know that, too.
I'm sure that I can be a help to you.

It concerns me that you won't appreciate
how much I can devote myself to you.

Pain burrs my throat. But why would I tear up
this way, if these were not my real feelings?

You don't know me, and I'm not deluded
into thinking we have met. But I can see

you also feel this needless separation,
as tear-stained in close-up you fade to black.

THE DOUBLE DEUCE

Patrick Swayze's seen it all before.
That's why he's the best. It's true, a bouncer
isn't typically your hero type,
but once he's oiled and practicing Tai Chi
across the lake from Ben Gazzara's house
his *pietas* shines forth like young Aeneas's.

Another town, another beery dive,
the same drunks making asses of themselves
in front of women who just want to drink
a Bud with friends and whisper to each other
about the new "cooler." He goes by Dalton.
A guy's ejected through the candy glass,

a rack of tumblers shatters on the bar.
One brawler takes a chair across the back
then crashes through a pasteboard tabletop.
And the blind guitarist plays his Squier Strat
with no mind paid to bursting bottles of beer
as they rain down on him. Hey, it's a gig.

As for Jeff Healey, who died way too young,
it's the gig of a lifetime, his guitar
laid flat across his lap, played from above.
He's singing "Long Tall Sally" with his band,
behind a chain link fence. This place is tough.
But Jeff knows Dalton's here to change all that.

He and Dalton go way back. They've been
in spots before, but none as tight as this one.
And Kelly Lynch is there, all blond and tan.
She plays a doctor who appreciates
a guy who's had his share of puncture wounds.
Her stubble-bearded Uncle Red's in trouble.

Enter Sam Elliott, who won't survive the film.
He holds his gray hair back with rubber bands
and flirts with Kelly charmingly. He's old
and knows this girl has plans for Dalton. *Mijo,*
he calls him—son, my bouncer son. They find
Sam on the bar dead drunk. No, no—just dead.

Well, Ben Gazzara's gotta pay for this.
His goons stabbed Sam and burned Red's auto parts
store to the ground. So Dalton drives the sleek
Diamond Blue Mercedes he's been babying
for the whole movie up to Ben Gazzara's.
He hates himself for tearing a man's throat out,

and now, god help him, he's done it again.
The Merc comes hurtling up Gazzara's lawn,
but it's a decoy. Dalton's in the house.
Then, following his lead, the cowering townsfolk
find their courage and a store of rifles
and blast Gazzara till his white shirt's red.

Glorious Gazzara. He's pure evil
and chews the scenery and smirks and dies
in a blaze of former-Cassavetes glory.
Swayze dies of cancer at 57.
The year that *Road House* came out ('89),
the Razzies nominated him worst actor.

Screw the Razzies, heartless wannabes.
I'd like to see them stand up for a neighbor
at great personal cost. They sip their
lattes in a strip mall in Van Nuys
and thumb their phones. Which one of them is going
to fight the man who's laid siege to their town?

after George Green

MOUSE DRAWER

I pull it open
slowly—
only the coiled
Victor loaded,
bent on springing.

Then, two black
beads stitched
on felt
climb the side
and see me.

The thing flutters
like a scoped heart,
then ducks back
down as I
kick it shut.

THUD

At some black hour we think we hear
THUD, like a dull instrument bruising
the ribs of the old house (new to us).

I say *think* because when, after I went
out in the rain in just my shorts,
following the flagstone walk that wraps

around the flower beds and lawn,
and found no tree trunk on the roof
and no thief's telltale of smashed glass,

I caught you outside in your nightgown
also at a loss for what caused
that low sound—more: we'd *felt* it.

But I was cold and, without proof,
began to lose the sense of it.
You were surer, too shaken to sleep.

That shook me, and so we lay
listening hard to the soft settling
a house carries on without our noticing.

TUMOR TREE

I'd cut it down, if it were mine,
to save the grass.
The tumors (I call them), when they
fall, get so you can't pass

the tree without a way so clogged
you have to step into the street
to get around these "oranges"
even raccoons won't eat.

I wonder what they think of it,
the owners we've never seen,
if they mind the pocked-up lawn.
Was it here when they moved in?

Though possibly I'd decide
I didn't want to lose the tree,
given the choice. Might be I'd want
it more if it belonged to me.

Some people like their tumors better
than what it takes to make them go,
or ending up with a useless stump.
And some just let their tumors grow.

OLD FRIENDS

They're bristly as a stand of winter wheat.
They slurp their soup and pinch your slice of bread
and, when you're in the can, softly repeat
the countless sins they level at your head.

All for love. You're thinking of them now:
the bag of snakes that makes up their good graces,
their fellowship a roiled ebb and flow
of blood staining their hypertensioned faces.

Be glad for what you've got, for they are it—
the ones you've known for ages, who've known you,
the living record of the little shit
you've been at times, an actual *Who's Who*

of who you've slept with, slights you've given, though
their own slights they just sweep behind the door.
But those tidbits are there for you to know,
holding their sins in trust, what friends are for.

SOURDOUGH

O tart mother,
frothy
source-barm,
rise.

Infuse me,
make me hoist,
torn and
palmed and
folded letter-wise.

You work your
spell in moments
of inattention
until I
am grown double,

ready for the fire,
breaking open
pungently
in the dark.

THE HUG

At Christmas dinner this year,
you remind your mother how she caught on fire
at the same dinner thirty years ago.
    The memory of it winds
around you like a bedsheet, as you see
her flounced, ivory cuff dip into the flame.

And when it came up changed,
it merely seemed a part of the hilarity,
her surprise and fluting voice, her sudden jerks
    like the aftermath of a joke
whose punch line you have to have repeated.
It happened out-of-time, a dolly zoom,

    till your father, then alive
(though not now for eleven Christmases),
saw the flame lurch up to take her arm.
    He stood amid the hoopla—
the twinkle lights and raised glasses of wine—
stepped toward her, and hugged the fire out.

    Behind our joyful talk,
we wish that he were here: the clear-eyed man
who could tell in a flash the difference
    between the lively
and the very life. Flame-lit, our faces flicker,
candles like stars reflected in black glass.

4 |

RAKING

for Mark Strand

Yesterday I heard
someone I knew—
not well, but liked—

had died, disease
unwinding him till
he was gone.

The horizon is scored
by a faint commotion—
vapor trails, cars,

but none are near.
The sky is milk white
and quiet here.

On the lawn, I fill
more black bags.
Almost all the leaves

are down. Winded
and warm, I drag them
to the curb.

THE ABLE MAN

A word in favor of the undeterred,
the heart-stiff, bluff, and dauntless perseverer
who warms to life, fully knowing it's absurd,
and even, as fiasco edges nearer,

takes pleasure in another round of drinks
or building bonds of trust or doing good
or whatever whirligigs his conscience thinks
will mollify the world and soothe his mood.

A thoughtful man, a braced-up citizen,
he does not pin his hopes on private wishes
but seeks the betterment of other men
and often helps his wife with doing dishes.

God bless him! Not for him the sudden veer
from puffed-up confidence down to the nadir
of pusillanimity, until your fear
hog-ties you like a backwoods home invader.

Now the one accomplishment that's left you
is simply to essay not to essay,
to make peace once your Lebenskraft's bereft you
and you live to fight (or not) another day.

PAPER WHITES

Gangling limbs
greened another inch
last night. You
note their growth

the way one
says a girl not
seen in weeks
has grown.

And in the gap
between the bulbs
you forced and
those you find

today, white stars
have come, cell
by cell, in no time.
You horse-shake

away a chill, agog
at the leggy
things already
starting to droop.

LET

Across the net,
she wilts and falls
behind, so I let
a few balls

slide by
in the midgy air
and drawn sky
of late summer.

Is this
letting her win
a Judas kiss—
the warm sin

of fooling too
far a daughter
who,
slow to laughter,

stakes all in all
on a game?
She's tall.
I call her name,

to snap her
back from the place
she goes, blur-
ring the odds: ace,

game, set.
Her stride returns,
as I abet
her. She learns

no lesson, nor
do I hint
at helping. After,
we sprint

on the road
home, our run
hung with gold
silk spun

by spiders in
patchy pines.
The threads glint
in sidewise lines,

cinches borne
by the air,
so loosely worn
they're hardly there.

LOW PRESSURE

He's still too small to fix the sail,
so I help him rig the rolling dinghy.
He wants to go off in the wind,
and before I can unhitch the bow
      he's heading out.
I like watching him scud along.
I suck air when he dips the rail
into the freezing current, jibing
hard or stuck in irons, trying
      to come about.

Keeping in harbor is the rule,
but it's still beyond where I can swim.
I call (too loud) when he's far enough.
I've got it, Dad, he hollers back
      into the breeze.
Worry tastes of bile, like rage.
He's learned how to read the wind
but doesn't know what wind can do
without warning and heedlessly.
      He has an ease

that makes my caution cowardly.
I see the bar he dares me with,
the rock that at low tide rides clear,
the seconds that stretch in the eye,
      the wave-washed pier.
What's the point? He can't hear me now.
He's scared of zombies, not of reefs,
his nightmares full of nothing real.
No use in saying the words I think,
      My dear, my dear.

Up High, No Higher

Up part way,
you clamber till

you're gone above
the muddy hill,

wedging your
upper thigh

against a crotch.
The blown sky

spills down
through jade,

leaf green tinting
green-leaf shade.

The topmost
boughs

flounce in
windy shows,

as your standing
leg quivers

then stops.
You see the river's

fuse lit from
the sun's banked spark.

The afternoon sifts
down to dark.

Dizzy and cold,
you jounce each

branch just
out of reach:

too high
and thin

for a kid
to climb in.

KEATS IN LOUISVILLE

His copy of Audubon's *Ornithology*
was worth a million dollars at his death,
to say nothing of his older brother's letters.
John dreamed of the New World but never saw it.
George, on the other hand, made the frontier his,
kept his coin close but paid the consumptive's debts.
Keats the businessman, Keats of Kentucky,
Keats for whom they named Keats Avenue,
a quarter mile of trees and clapboard houses.
The one Keats brother to outlive his twenties,
he kept three slaves and died at forty-four.

PAN AM

ABC, Fall 2011

A torn TV poster
with five soap-fresh faces
and ten legs *passant*
in stewardess blue.

All feed hopes
for their new-fledged lives
(the actresses, too),
unaware that the plug

was yanked at the network
weeks ago due
to soft commitment
and busted luck.

Lack of belief
was not their failing.
Just look at this ad—
so coltish, so bluff.

Even so, it ended,
despite their ardor,
our costly story,
cast in dreams,

of who we were then—
heralds of the busy air
and of long sky views—
slowly setting down.

Last Job

We finished school in May. I headed east.
You moved back home. We talked by phone. You came
to visit once and stayed in a hotel.
But the city wasn't going to work for you:
too tall, too many steam holes, too much noise.

Months before, we'd robbed a bookstore where
you'd been made manager. You had the keys.
With my blue Buick idling outside,
we helped ourselves to boxes full of books,
walked them right out the front door: poetry,
a book on flying, Kafka's stories, pulp.
Books were our thing. We loved them, and we felt
they should be ours, God knows why. So we took
what we could while it was ours to take.

THE FACULTY ABROAD

The term is done, the grades are in,
the pensions booked—ten nights, nine days.
The touring faculty begin
their transatlantic getaways
to Paris or swank ateliers
in Venice or in Amsterdam.
So you, too, can enjoy their stays,
they post the proof on Instagram.

Beneath the Mona Lisa's chin,
one shyly grins, while others gaze
at selfies by Rembrandt van Rijn.
Mein Gott, the *food*: torched crème brûlées,
a sautéed quail in demi-glaze,
zuppa inglese, Black Forest ham.
It's true, they know the best cafés.
They post the proof on Instagram.

#Europe, ftw!
They've gone to slough off their malaise,
disguising they're Amerikin
by slyly looking up the phrase
for "May I have some mayonnaise?"
The Old World sets the bar for glam:
they love to try out their bidets.
They post the proof on Instagram.

Lest we miss their new berets
and so the stay-at-home mesdames
et messieurs can heap them up with praise,
they post the proof on Instagram.